SIMPLE & EASY
LARGE FLOWER
COLORING BOOK

FOR SENIORS : BEGINNERS : LOW VISION

Simple & Easy Large Coloring Book
For Seniors : Beginners : Low Vision

Copyright © Alcovia Co Publishing

First Edition, November 2020

ISBN: 9798563218932

Peonies

Roses

Sunflower

Orchids

Lilies

Hibiscus

Pansies

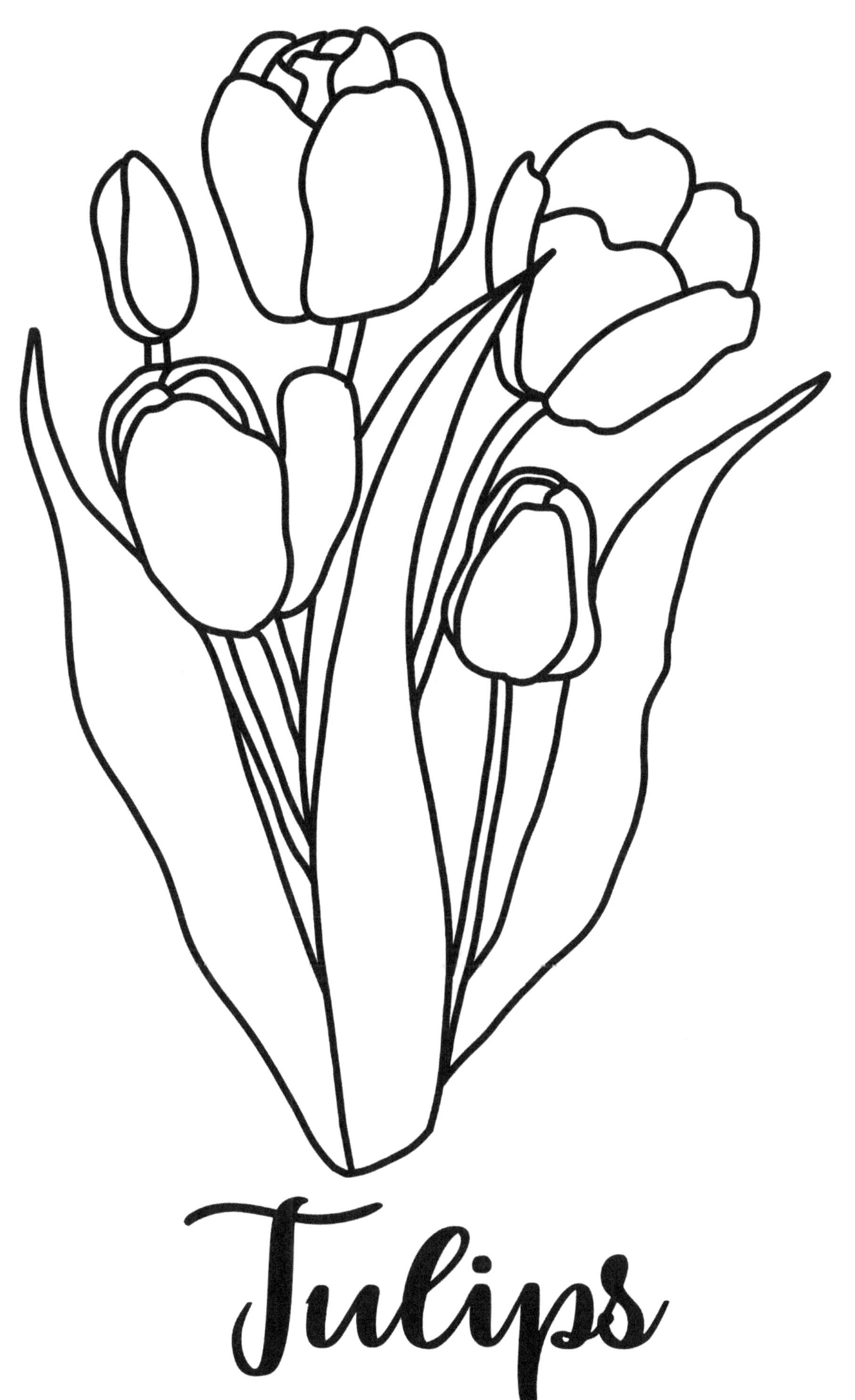

Tulips

Daffodils

Carnations

Iris

Cyclamen

Poppies

Violets

Mimosa

Hyacinth

Anemone

Gladiolus

Hydrangea

Bluebells

Forget-me-not

Bougainvillea

Buttercup

Camelia

Chrysanthemum

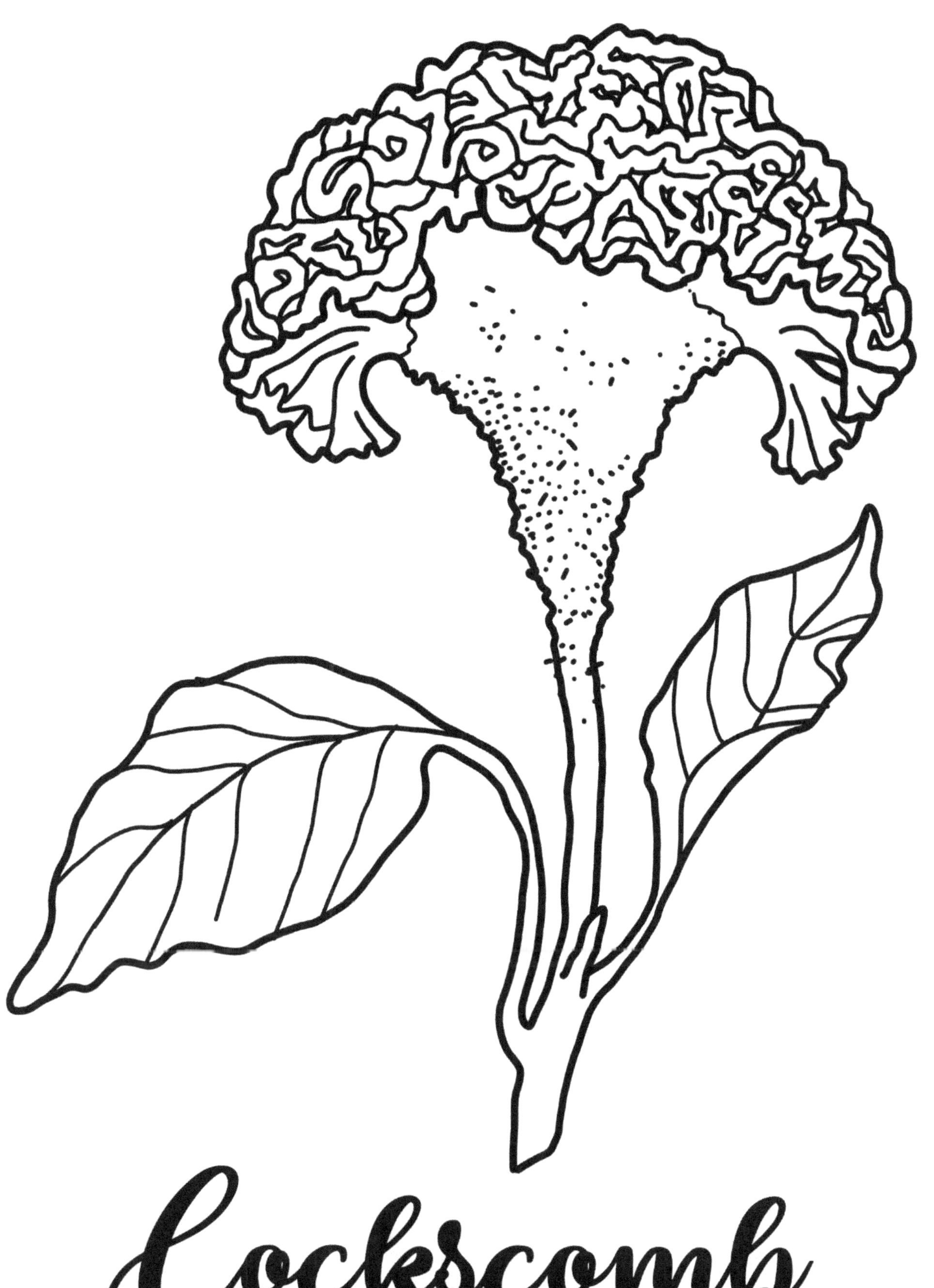

Cockscomb

Confederate Rose

Crocus

Dahlia

Eglatine

Flamboyant

Foxglove

Geranium

Geranium

Lavender

Lilac

Lotus

Magnolia

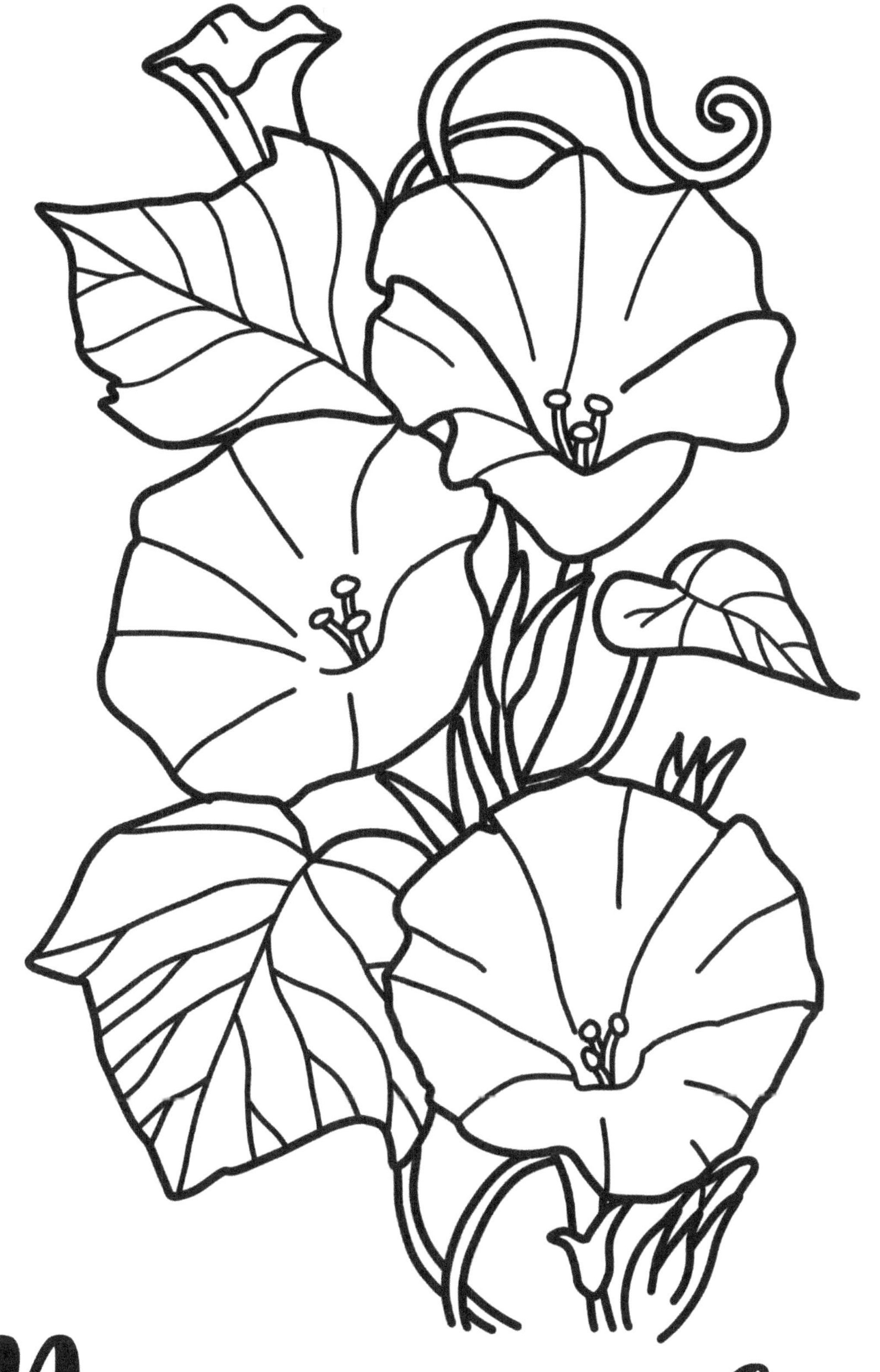

Morning glory

Dandelions

Primrose

Balloon Flower

Amaryllis

Aster

Begonia

Periwinkle

Moss Rose

Zinnia

Anthurium

Cherry Blossom